COVENTRY LIBRARIES

Please return this book on or before
the last date stamped below.

To renew this book take it to any of
the City Libraries before
the date due for return

Coventry City Council

USBORNE TRUE STORIES

POLAR
ADVENTURES

USBORNE TRUE STORIES

POLAR ADVENTURES

BY PAUL DOWSWELL

First published in 2018 by Usborne Publishing Ltd.,
Usborne House, 83-85 Saffron Hill, London EC1N 8RT, England.
www.usborne.com

Copyright © Usborne Publishing 2018

Illustrations copyright © Usborne Publishing, 2018

The name Usborne and the devices ♀ 🎈 are Trade Marks of
Usborne Publishing Ltd. UE

A CIP catalogue record for this book is available from the British Library.

CONTENTS

CHAPTER 1

THE TOP AND BOTTOM OF THE WORLD

If you have a globe, spin it around. The two places where your globe is anchored to its stand are the North and South Poles – the top and bottom of the world – once thought to be as unreachable as distant planets. Until the early 20th century, no one had ventured that far. What an explorer would actually find at these two spots was a mystery. Would these Poles provide an entrance into new worlds inside our planet? What strange creatures might live in such hostile surroundings?

But the Poles are just positions on a map: an invention of science marked by a reading of 90° north or 90° south, based on a system of map coordinates known as latitude and longitude. As actual places, they are unremarkable. When he got to the South Pole in 1912, explorer Robert Falcon Scott noted with some disappointment that there was, "very little that is different from the awful monotony of past days."

The North Pole is surrounded by the Arctic, a huge frozen ocean containing an assortment of bleak islands. In the days before whole continents and oceans could be captured in a single satellite photograph, it proved fatally difficult to map and explore. Although the Arctic had been visited by European traders and settlers for more than 1,000 years, it wasn't until the early 20th century that a detailed map of its icy core was completed.

The first serious attempts to explore the Arctic were driven by the need to discover a sea route from Europe to China and other Far Eastern

Map of the North Pole

countries. There were two main ways around the Arctic: northeast above the coast of Russia, or northwest through the Canadian Arctic. Here, Europeans came into contact with people called Inuit – once known as Eskimos. Many early explorers regarded the Inuit as living in the Stone

9

Age, but their ability to adapt and survive in such a region showed great ingenuity.

The first expeditions faced terrifying dangers and invariably ended in starvation, mutiny and death. The Russian Admiralty made progress though, with a series of expeditions between 1733 and 1743, which mapped out the entire Arctic coast of Russia, from the Atlantic to the Pacific.

At that time, the Arctic coast of Canada west of the Hudson Bay was still virtually unknown. This was to change in the first half of the 19th century, when British explorers made repeated efforts to open up the Northwest Passage. Sir John Franklin's expedition of 1845-1848 was a disaster. His ships were lost and all his crew died. Over the next 10 years, 40 expeditions were launched to find him. Although his ships were never found, in the course of their travels his would-be rescuers began to understand more about this complex region.

The discovery and exploration of Antarctica, the vast continent where the South Pole is located, was simpler. Unlike the Arctic, it isn't surrounded by such a maze of islands. Although it was only sighted for the first time in 1820, for a couple of hundred years before this explorers had guessed there was an 'uninhabited land' to the far south. Antarctica is twice the size of Australia. In places, land lies beneath a layer of ice 4km (2.5 miles) deep.

The great age of polar exploration took place in the years before the First World War. In the Arctic, adventurers advanced steadily towards the top of the world. In the Antarctic, seafarers believed they could build ships strong enough to withstand the crushing ice fields that surround the continent – although they were sometimes mistaken. In these early days, radio and aircraft were such new inventions that their use was barely considered. Instead, polar explorers spent months at sea before reaching these unknown lands. Then, they ventured inland knowing that if anything went wrong, they'd be beyond rescue.

So many things could go wrong, it was, perhaps,

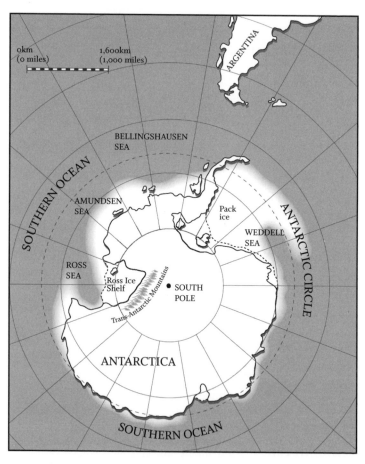

Map of the South Pole

astonishing that anyone went at all. The cold
pierced them to the bone. Even the strongest ships
could be caught in pack ice and crushed to
matchsticks. At the Poles, midwinter is marked by

days of constant dark. The endless darkness drove men insane.

Lack of fresh fruit and vegetables in their diet led to scurvy – a horrible disorder which affected all seafarers until the early 20th century. It makes its victims feel as though they're being eaten away from the inside. Their gums turn black and their teeth drop out. Their arms and legs swell up, their joints ache and their skin is covered with livid rashes and ulcers, which ooze blood and pus. Scurvy attacks the body's weakest points. Fresh wounds never heal. Old wounds, long since healed, open up again. Captain Scott's famous expedition, for example, was fatally hindered by it.

The men also suffered from frostbite. Body tissues in exposed parts of the body, such as the hands, toes, noses and ears, freeze, preventing blood from reaching them. Deprived of its blood supply, skin and flesh dies. When the affected area thaws, the victim suffers extreme pain. Left untreated, frostbite can turn to gangrene: the flesh rots, poisoning the whole body. Frostbite remains one of the greatest threats to explorers of both Poles. It affects modern-explorers just as it did adventurers in the 16th century.

Today, it's possible to book a trip to the North or South Pole. You can stand on the exact spot that marks either Pole before hopping aboard a warm plane or icebreaker which will take you back to civilization in a matter of hours. One travel company even drops clients off at a point where they ski the final few miles to their destination, to be met by a plane for the return journey.

Such comfortable tales of hi-tech adventure are not typical, however. Almost a century ago, British explorer Apsley Cherry-Garrard famously said: "Polar exploration is at once the cleanest, most isolated way of having a bad time which has ever been devised." – as you'll find out in the stories in this book...

CHAPTER 2

THE POLARIS MYSTERY

How Charles Hall's wife must have regretted the day he picked up a book about Sir John Franklin and his lost expedition. The story sparked an interest in the Arctic that would frequently take her husband away on long expeditions, and eventually leave her a penniless widow, with a 10-year-old son who'd barely seen his father.

Hall's interest in Franklin increased when he heard Lady Franklin speak about her ill-fated husband in the Halls' home town of Cincinnati, USA, in 1849. Eleven years later, in 1860, Hall had raised enough money to embark on a two-year exploration of the southeast coast of Baffin Island, to search for the remains of Franklin's expedition.

Hall was not an adventurer by profession. He made his living as a newspaper publisher. The only known photograph of him shows an intense, heavily built man with a huge, bushy beard.

On his trip to Baffin Island, he met Tookolito and Ebierbing, an Inuit couple who'd been taken to London in the 1850s. There, they'd learned to speak English, and adopted the manners and fashions of polite English society. They'd been a sensation in both Britain and America, but eventually returned to Baffin Island. They were to feature heavily in Hall's future, as would Sidney Budington, captain of the ship that took him north.

Two years after the Baffin Island trip, Hall set off on another epic expedition in search of Franklin. This time he was away for five years, and returned with a few relics from a previous British expedition – mainly sacks of coal. But what Hall really wanted to do was travel to the North Pole. Over the years, this ambition grew into an obsession. He was, he declared, "born to discover the North Pole. Once I have set my right foot on the Pole I shall be perfectly willing to die."

Like all explorers, he needed money to get there, and in 1870 Hall managed to persuade the US government to back him. He was given a Navy tug which he named *Polaris* – another name for the North Star, which lies almost directly above the North Pole. He spent $50,000 transforming the tug into a formidable Arctic ship, strong enough to withstand the ice and storms it would face.

No polar explorer could have hoped for a better ship, but sadly the same could not be said of its crew. The extreme conditions and dangers of polar exploration called for men who were team players with boundless optimism and common decency – qualities that most of Hall's crew entirely lacked.

First, he picked Sidney Budington as captain. Once a respected whaling captain, but now a secret drinker, Budington didn't even like Hall. He also had no interest in reaching the Pole, but was probably grateful for the work. Next, Hall hired two other former sea captains as senior officers on the ship: Hubbard Chester and George Tyson.

To secure funds from the US government, Hall also agreed to bring several scientists along, to keep records and collect rocks, plants and animals. Chief among them was a respected, but forbidding, German academic and surgeon, Dr. Emil Bessels. Another German, Frederick Meyer, was the expedition meteorologist – a weather expert. Hall resented having the scientists on board, fearing that their work would interfere with his own ambition to reach the Pole, but he had little choice.

The crew also included Tookolito, Ebierbing and their young son, and a large number of German sailors. Later, when the *Polaris* stopped off in Greenland, they were joined by another Inuit couple with their three children.

The *Polaris* sailed from New York in July 1871.

Just before departure, Hall declared their future would be 'glorious'. George Tyson, on the other hand, wrote in his journal a week later: "I see there is not perfect harmony between Captain Hall and the Scientific Corp, nor with some others either. I am afraid things will not work well."

Hall's inexperience as a leader showed at every turn. Almost immediately, he fell out with the scientists, and then with Budington, who'd started raiding the storeroom for medicinal alcohol to feed his addiction. Budington, Chester and Tyson, all experienced sea captains, saw each other as rivals. Meanwhile, the Germans, Americans and Inuit each formed cliques, rarely mixing with each other.

Yet, despite the heated arguments and open animosity, the voyage began well. Good weather ensured remarkable progress. By August 29, the ship had passed through the narrow channel that separates Greenland from Ellesmere Island. Here, existing maps came to an end, and they began to record unknown territory. In early September, the

Polaris reached 82° North. Ahead lay a clear sea, and the promise of more fine weather, but Budington had now gone as far north as he was prepared to go. He knew that the further they went, the more difficult it would be to get back.

Autumn was approaching. The crew settled in a bay in newly named Hall Land, in northern Greenland, to wait out the winter. Hall called their mooring 'Thank God Harbor'. (Both these place names remain to this day.) When the ice had frozen around their ship, Hall gave his men a pep talk: "You have left your homes, friends, and country; indeed, you have bid a long farewell for a time to the whole civilized world, for the purpose of aiding me in discovering the mysterious, hidden parts of the earth." When spring came, he told them, they would head north.

So far, Hall had been lucky. His crew had worked together so long as there had been good weather. They were reasonably warm and well fed, and there was plenty to keep them occupied. The coming months, when they would be stuck in bleak, monotonous surroundings, with dark winter nights, blizzards and gales, would test them all to the limit.

Sure enough, before the year was out, disaster struck. Hall's health had never been good, and previous Arctic expeditions had taken their toll. The first sign came in October. On an exploratory sled trip, Hall forgot to pack several vital pieces of equipment. A companion had to be sent back to the *Polaris* to fetch warm clothing, a stove and a navigation instrument which they would need to find their way back to the ship. Hall's mind was failing him fast.

When Hall returned two weeks later, he complained about his inability to keep up with the dogs. He'd often had to ride on the sled. Physical as well as mental weakness was overtaking him. As soon as he came aboard he drank a cup of coffee, and was violently sick. Confined to his bed, he became delirious and began to accuse his companions of poisoning him.

In early November, Hall seemed to make a startling recovery. He raised himself from his bed to work on his journal, but all was not well. He was distracted, and would lose track of what he was saying. Paralysis set in, and his eyes took on a doomed, glassy appearance. On November 8, 1871, he slipped into unconsciousness, and died. He was buried close to the ship in the cold, pebble ground of Thank God Harbor.

His death is a mystery to this day. He could have suffered a stroke, or a heart attack – both ailments have similar symptoms – but he could also have been poisoned. Arsenic produces similar effects to both these illnesses. In the 1960s, a biographer of Hall's asked for permission to visit the grave and examine the body. Hall was duly dug up and found to be fairly well-preserved – as bodies generally are in such cold conditions. Samples of hair and fingernails were removed and sent to a laboratory in Montreal, which specialized in the examination of long-dead bodies. Tests showed conclusively that

Hall had ingested a large quantity of arsenic. But had he been murdered?

Given the ill-feeling between Hall, his captain and the scientists, it's possible one of them had decided to kill him. Bessels, as a doctor, was a prime suspect. Perhaps he thought they'd be free to carry out their work more efficiently with Hall out of the way. Budington, too, could have poisoned him, because he didn't wish to take the ship any further north.

Arsenic, in small doses, was a common medicine in the late 19th century. It was a standard ingredient in remedies for indigestion, from which Hall suffered. So perhaps Hall had simply had a heart attack or massive stroke, and trusting no one, had tried to treat himself from his own medicine supply, accidentally giving himself an overdose of arsenic. We shall never know.

With Hall gone, control of the expedition passed to Budington, who'd already made it clear that he thought the whole trip was a waste of time. Taking command didn't change his view. The spirits of his already divided crew sank dramatically.

Before he died, Hall had made some successful efforts at uniting the men. He established a regular Sunday religious service, which had provided an opportunity for all the crew to come together. It had also been a weekly ritual that marked the passage of time. But this was now abandoned. The crew's winter existence became formless, and the days and weeks slipped into an unmarked void. Budington made other, seemingly bizarre, decisions. The men were all issued with firearms, the idea being that if any animal came by – a stray bird or a lone seal – it could be shot for food whenever the chance arose. The prospect of a fractious, divided crew, all carrying weapons, was an alarming one.

The atmosphere on the *Polaris* plummeted further when some of the crew broke into the scientists' alcohol supplies. Both officers and men would terrorize the ship in drunken rampages. It was difficult enough to get by in the endless polar winter, but now everyone's nerves were in tatters.

Then the ship's carpenter, Nathaniel Coffin, went insane. Convinced the rest of the crew was trying to murder him in the most gruesome ways, he would never sleep in the same spot. Instead, he wandered around the decks and passageways of the ship, muttering or raving according to his mood.

Winter passed, but spring brought no thaw. Fortunately, some animals returned, so there was no danger of starvation. By midsummer, however, there was still no sign that the ice would crack and allow them to escape.

Then, on August 12, 1872, two events occurred to brighten their dreary existence. One of the Inuit women, who'd come aboard at Greenland, gave birth to a baby. This was a total surprise to everyone except her and her husband, as her swollen belly had been concealed by her bulky, seal-skin clothing. The baby was named Charles Polaris, after the dead commander and his ship.

On that same day, the ice broke up, and the

Polaris set out to sea after nearly a year at Thank God Harbor.

However, their luck didn't last. Within three days they were stuck fast in pack ice once again, but at least this ice was slowly drifting south.

As the nights grew longer and the supply of wildlife to hunt grew scarce, the crew had to accept that they were in for another Arctic winter. By now, the *Polaris* was leaking, and precious coal was being used to keep the ship's pumps working to clear the hold of seawater. An argument between Budington and his crew, over whether they should pump water by hand to save coal, ended with a cabin door being slammed in his face. These tensions were to grow worse. Much worse.

On October 15, during a terrible storm, the ice around the *Polaris* was hit by a huge iceberg. In the panic, Budington ordered two lifeboats and some crates of supplies to be lowered overboard. After four hours, however, it became clear that *Polaris* had not been too badly damaged after all.

George Tyson was on the ice, helping to supervise the unloading of the ship. He and Budington had a heated shouting match from ship to ice, about whether to load the boats and supplies back onto *Polaris*. Budington, strangely, ordered the men on the ice to move these items even further away from the ship. While Tyson pondered this peculiar order, the ice surrounding the ship began to crack. As the snow whirled around their heads, and the wind tossed the angry, swirling sea, the men on the ice watched *Polaris* drift beyond their reach and vanish into the night.

Morning came and the storm passed. The 19 members of the *Polaris* stranded on the ice now had the chance to examine their new home. In other circumstances they might have been charmed by their surroundings. The floe was like a miniature island. There were lakes of fresh water, formed by melted snow, and little hillocks. Altogether, the ice was about 6km (4 miles) in circumference.

Tyson, as the most senior officer, was supposed to be in command, but he faced an impossible task. His fellow castaways, already a divided bunch, would be driven even further apart by their terrible situation. When the *Polaris* had lurched away from the ice, Budington, Bessels and 12 of the crew were still on board. Here on the floe, Tyson had Frederick Meyer, most of the Germans, the two Inuit couples and their five children, including new baby Charles. The Germans seemed to regard Meyer as their leader, but his authority was shaky. To make matters worse, he and Tyson didn't get along.

The castaways created two separate camps. The Germans set up tents, and the Inuit built igloos for themselves, Tyson and the other crewmen.

In circumstances such as these, people stand a much better chance of survival if they work together, helping the weakest and conserving supplies, but Tyson couldn't get the German sailors to cooperate. They would raid his food supply, often stuffing their faces until they were sick.

They even burned one of the boats to keep warm, and stole some of his clothing. However, when the *Polaris* had broken away, the German sailors had been carrying their guns, and he had not. There was nothing he could do to enforce his control.

Fortunately, one group among them was prepared to help them all. Starvation that winter was prevented thanks mainly to the Inuits' hunting skills. By some miracle, no one died and no one killed anyone. Then, just as the worst seemed to be over and the survivors could begin to look forward to spring, the floe began to break up.

By the middle of March, their little world had shrunk to a fraction of what it had been before, and it was getting smaller by the day. Towering icebergs surrounded them, threatening to smash the shrinking floe into ice splinters. There was nothing left to do but take to the remaining boat, and cramming 19 people into a rowing boat meant for eight wasn't easy.

The nightmare journey that followed would

haunt them for the rest of their lives. In heaving seas of ice and mountainous waves, the tiny, overloaded boat battled against the freezing wind to reach land. The crew grew weaker by the hour through lack of food and fresh water.

On April 8, when a crack unexpectedly opened on the edge of a floe they were resting on, Meyer fell into the freezing sea. Ebierbing, and another Inuit named Hans, ran out through wobbling chunks of ice to pull him out. The shock of falling into sub-zero water almost killed Meyer. He stopped breathing and would have died, if Hans hadn't pummelled his body until he regained consciousness. The fall crushed his spirit, and left him frostbitten and feverish.

Recalling his appearance in the following days, Tyson wrote: "He is very tall and thin. If [an artist] had wanted a model to stand for Famine, he might have drawn Meyer… He was the most wretched-looking object I ever saw." Tyson feared that Meyer's decline would bring him further trouble.

Meyer had had some authority over his fellow Germans, but as he grew weaker, it all but evaporated.

In their darkest hour, the men seemed to rediscover their humanity. On the evening of April 19, the castaways made camp on a floe, until a fierce storm broke, and torrents of water swamped their icy refuge. The men bundled the Inuit women and children into the boat, and held onto their slippery perch as best they could. After each wave washed over them, they would haul the boat back into the middle of the ice floe and wait for the next onslaught.

In the early morning light, they could see the floe was melting into the sea, and the boat was launched. A strange silence fell over the usually mutinous crew. Stunned by their narrow escape and the horror of their circumstances, they finally looked to Tyson for leadership, and readily obeyed his every command.

In the days that followed, the weather grew

worse. Of the wind and the sea, Tyson wrote in his journal: "They played with us and our boat as if we were shuttlecocks." Reviewing their situation, he concluded: "Half-drowned we are, and cold enough in our wet clothes, without shelter, and not sun enough to dry us even on the outside. We have nothing to eat; everything is finished and gone. The prospect looks bad."

But the situation was not as bad as Tyson imagined. By now, they had drifted far enough south to have reached the usual limits of the whale and seal ships that roamed the Arctic. They sighted their first ship on the afternoon of April 28. This must have been the moment when everyone on board allowed themselves to hope that they might survive after all. But fate had not finished with them yet.

The first two ships they sighted didn't see their frantic signals. It was only on the morning of April 30 that they were finally rescued, by a Newfoundland sealer called the *Tigress*.

Safely back home in the United States, Tyson

learned of the fate of the *Polaris*. The men on board had fared little better than those stranded on the ice floe. As the ship floated away, it had sprung a serious leak, and Budington had been forced to land on the west coast of Smith Sound. As they no longer had any lifeboats, the crew had to take apart their vessel to build smaller boats. They used these to travel down the coast until they reached the whale and seal hunting grounds, where they were rescued by a Scottish whaler.

When news of Hall's disastrous expedition broke, it caused a sensation and a scandal. It read, after all, like a cross between a boy's adventure story and a psychological murder mystery. The ordeal of the Inuit women and children provoked particular sympathy among American newspaper readers, and the Inuit families were inundated with gifts of bundles of clothing.

But there were serious questions to be answered. The United States government launched an inquiry into the loss of the ship and the death of its commander, but it was difficult to piece together any clear picture among all the conflicting accounts. If any dirty deeds had been done, neither the officers nor the crew were willing to admit them. The Board of Inquiry decided that Hall had died of a stroke. Despite the discovery of arsenic traces when his body was exhumed in the 1960s, there is still no solid evidence to suggest he was murdered, and no obvious prime suspect.

FROM 1873 TO 1908

Charles Hall's disastrous failure and the terrible hardships faced by his crew merely whetted the appetite of other explorers to do better.

In 1879, an American expedition, led by Lieutenant Commander George Washington De Long, set sail through the Bering Strait, off the eastern Siberian coast, in the ship *Jeanette*. The ship was caught in ice and drifted for 22 months, before sinking. When wreckage from the *Jeanette* drifted over to Greenland, Norwegian explorer Fridtjof Nansen hit on the idea of reaching the North Pole by drifting there in a strong ship.

The *Fram* (which means 'forward') was designed to resist crushing by ice. During its three-year journey from 1893 to 1896, Nansen and his crew gained vast amounts of knowledge about the Arctic. They established once and for all that the North Pole was just part of a huge icy sea, rather than solid land. Nansen and a colleague left the *Fram* to sled and ski their way to the North Pole, but failed, and had to be rescued. In the early 1900s, American, German, Swedish and Italian teams all crept closer to the Pole, and it seemed only a matter of time before someone would reach it.

At the same time, efforts were also being made to reach the Antarctic. Between 1898 and 1899, an international team aboard the Belgian ship *Belgica* were trapped in ice, and became the first people to winter south of the Antarctic Circle.

A year later, a British expedition under Carsten E. Borchgrevink spent the winter on the continent itself, at Cape Adare. It was the British who made the greatest progress exploring the Antarctic. Captain Robert Falcon Scott, from 1901 to 1904, and Sir Ernest Shackleton, from 1907 to 1909, both led sled parties deep into the heart of Antarctica. The two became rivals, and it seemed certain that one of them would be the first explorer to reach the South Pole.

CHAPTER 3

"WON AT LAST BY THE STARS AND STRIPES"

More often than not, success is not half as interesting as failure. When the North Pole was finally conquered, the story of the first team to reach it was notably lacking in drama – apart from the murder of one of the party. What happened afterwards was far more interesting.

The man usually credited with being the first to reach the North Pole was US Navy engineer Robert Peary. A tall, wiry man, he was already the most famous Arctic explorer of his age. In almost all his photographs he stares out at the world with scorn. A lifetime dedicated to reaching the North Pole had turned him into a rather unpleasant person. Yet, from such arrogance and self-belief, heroes are often made.

Peary's accounts of his trips make much of the hardship of polar exploration. His own courage couldn't be doubted. During an Arctic expedition in 1898, he lost nine toes to gangrene brought on by frostbite. Thereafter, he walked with a curious sliding step, but it didn't put him off Arctic travel.

The journey that Peary claimed took him to the North Pole began in 1908. He'd already been to the Arctic six times before; his last trip, in 1906, taking him less than two hundred miles from the Pole. Peary had learned a lot from these journeys. He designed his own sleds, stoves and clothing, all based closely on tried and trusted designs. He slept in the open, as many Inuit did, and only built an igloo when the temperature dropped to extreme levels. He even ate some of his food cold, gnawing on frozen 'pemmican' – dried meat and fat pounded into a paste. After all, eating uncooked food saved on fuel.

Peary chose the members of his team not only for their character, but also for their size – small, wiry men who needed less food than big, tall men, and took up less space in an igloo. His ship, the *Roosevelt*, was built on similar principles. It was short, to make it easier to steer, and its tough wooden sides were 76cm (30 inches) thick – strong enough to survive crushing Arctic ice. It was the only vessel in North America built especially for the northernmost reaches of the Arctic Ocean.

When he set off, at the age of 52, Peary had already spent much of his life exploring the region. His age was against him, his health was shaky, and the people who funded his adventures were impatient for a success after so many failures. He must have known this was going to be his last chance. After a grand send-off from New York, on July 6, 1908, the *Roosevelt* headed for Cape

Columbia on Ellesmere Island's northern coast. Supplies were unloaded and the expedition made their winter headquarters. Before the winter came, sled parties were sent off to lay down supplies on the route north.

On February 28, 1909, 24 men set out with 133 dogs and 19 sleds, each carrying a vast weight of supplies. Peary's plan was for them all to head north, and then return to base, sled by sled, as their food and fuel supplies were used up.

Right from the start, the going across the ice was exceptionally good. It was very cold that season, and the ice had frozen hard – ideal conditions for sleds. The only problems they encountered were when huge 'leads' (cracks in the ice which left gaps of water) opened up in the trail before them. Sometimes they had to wait several days for a lead to close before they could continue north.

For Peary, everything went brilliantly well. But for others on his party, the story was not so rosy. One of his colleagues, an American named Ross

Marvin, was said to have fallen into a hole in the ice and drowned. The truth, when it came out, was much messier. Marvin had two Inuit with him, whom he had driven on relentlessly. One of them had repeatedly asked to rest on a sled, but Marvin had refused. Finally, the man had killed Marvin and dumped his body under the ice.

As Peary's men neared their destination, all that remained of the original party was Peary himself, his servant Henson, four Inuit, five sleds and 40 dogs. Peary claimed to have reached the Pole on April 6, 1909, at around one o'clock in the afternoon, and stayed there some 30 hours.

It was an historic occasion, remembered with a typical lack of modesty by Peary, who summed it up like this: "The discovery of the North Pole stands for the inevitable victory of courage, persistence, endurance, over all obstacles… The discovery of [this]… splendid, frozen jewel of the north, for which through centuries men of every nation have struggled, and suffered and died, is won at last, and is won forever, by the Stars and Stripes!" It was undoubtedly an important moment: "The closing of the book on 400 years of history," according to Peary, further blowing his own trumpet.

Peary and his companions raced back to Cape Columbia. The journey to the Pole had taken them 40 days. The return took a mere 16. Navigating through a sea of fractured ice, the *Roosevelt* sailed for home. By September 6, they'd reached Indian Harbor, Labrador. Here, Peary sent four messages – to his wife Josephine, to The *New York Times*, to the Associated Press news agency, and to the Peary Arctic Club, the organization he'd set up to fund his polar ambitions.

It was also here, however, that Peary discovered something that was to sour his sense of triumph. Four days earlier, another American, named Frederick Cook, had announced to the world that he had reached the Pole too – and that he had arrived a whole year earlier.

CHAPTER 4

THE INFAMOUS DR. COOK

Peary's rival was a likeable doctor of medicine named Frederick Cook, who worked in Brooklyn. The two men knew each other well and had sailed for the Arctic together over 1891-1892. Like Peary, Cook saw being first to the Pole as an opportunity for world-wide fame, but he lacked Peary's prestigious and wealthy backers, so he set out to raise funds by bringing an Inuit couple to the United States and taking them on a lecture tour. This was exactly the same tactic that Charles Hall had used, and it worked. Public interest in the polar regions was high. They were, after all, among the last places on earth still unvisited. Audiences flocked to see Cook and his Inuit, and were fascinated by the ingenious construction of Inuit sleds, their fur and animal-skin clothing, and kayaks made of seal bone and skin.

Cook was well known to other explorers. He'd led a cruise to the Arctic which had gone disastrously wrong. His passengers, who had paid $500 apiece to come along, endured mutiny and a sinking ship. They still enjoyed the adventure, though, and celebrated their ordeal by forming 'The Arctic Club', which became one of New York's most prestigious societies for explorers.

Cook had also been aboard the *Belgica* (see page 36). Norwegian polar explorer Roald Amundsen was among the crew too, and wrote of Cook: "[He was] a man of unfaltering courage, unfailing hope, endless cheerfulness, and unwearied kindness."

Fame followed in 1903, when Cook announced

that he'd climbed Mount McKinley, the highest peak in North America. He wrote a best-selling book about it, *To the Top of the Continent*, and was elected president of the *American Explorer's Club*. Unlike Peary, Cook seemed to be a good-natured person. Photographs show him with a twinkle in his eye, as if he's about to say something amusing.

Unfortunately, all this was to change. Such was the disgrace heaped on Cook in the years to come, that he described himself as 'the most shamefully abused man in the history of exploration'. That may have been true, but there was also something in his character which led him astray, and which would, in the end, destroy his reputation as a great explorer.

Cook's downfall began in 1907, when he set off from New York to try to reach the North Pole. The trip was financed by John R. Bradley, a wealthy American gambling-club owner and big-game hunter who'd become a friend. Bradley suggested they keep the voyage secret, so that if Cook failed they could pass off the trip as a hunting expedition.

Cook sailed to the Arctic Circle aboard a ship named the *John R. Bradley* after his backer. Bradley came along too, intending to add walruses and polar bears to his collection of stuffed animals.

Bradley couldn't help boasting about his voyage, so news of Cook's forthcoming attempt on the Pole reached Peary while the ship was holed up in dry dock, undergoing repairs. Peary was angry and worried. He'd put so much effort into trying to reach the Pole, he felt he was entitled to do so without anyone else trying to get there before him.

Cook, and the ship's cook Rudolph Francke, were dropped off by the *John R. Bradley* in the Inuit village of Anoatok, near Etah, Greenland. After spending the winter there, the two of them set off for the Pole, together with nine Inuit. At first they went west, crossed Ellesmere Island, and reached the tip of Axel Heiberg Island where they left a large supply dump. On March 18, they headed north across the frozen Arctic Ocean on a thousand mile round trip to the North Pole.

For this daring leap into the unknown, Cook took only two other people: Ahwelah and Etukishook, accompanied by two sleds and 26 dogs. Francke, stricken with scurvy, had given up, as had seven of the Inuit. According to Cook, they covered the five hundred miles to the top of the world in 34 days, claiming to have reached the Pole on April 21, 1908 – almost a year before Peary.

The return journey was harrowing. Cook's party was gone for 14 months with only two months' supply of food. They shot polar bears and seals to eat when they could, but at several points they were so starved they resorted to eating candles, and even the leather straps of their sleds.

Once Cook's party reached the fringes of human habitation in Greenland, they took a boat to Scandinavia via the Shetland Islands. Here, on September 2, 1909, Cook sent a telegram announcing his triumph to the world. Then he headed for the Danish capital, Copenhagen, where he was greeted by a pack of journalists. The Danes hailed him as a great hero, and heaped awards upon him. He was given a gold medal from the *Danish Royal Geographical Society*, and an honorary degree by the University of Copenhagen – but Cook wasn't allowed to enjoy his fame for long.

During a celebratory banquet, a telegraph arrived with news of Peary's claim to have been the first to the Pole. This had been announced on September 6, four days after Cook's own message to the world. An extraordinary photograph was taken moments after the telegraph was read out. The diners, dressed in stiff white shirts and formal dinner jackets, look stunned. Some stare accusingly at Cook. One man is puffing out his cheeks in astonishment. Cook stands in the middle, a garland of flowers draped around his dinner jacket. He wears an almost comical expression of disappointment and surprise.

Who would the world believe? Unfortunately for Cook, Peary was well placed to win the argument. He was funded by the American

Museum of Natural History, and some of the richest and most respected men in America. He had the blessing of the *National Geographic Society*, and had even lunched with President Roosevelt (after whom he'd named his ship) before he'd set off. The *New York Times* supported him too.

Cook, meanwhile, was backed by a disreputable big-game hunter who'd made his fortune from gambling. Cook had also returned with no written account of his journey, claiming he'd left all his records in the Arctic. Then, his companions, Ahwelah and Etukishook, confessed that in all their time with Cook they'd never been out of sight of land. They also claimed that a photograph supposedly showing them at the Pole had been taken on top of an igloo, two days' march from land. A final blow to his reputation came when it was revealed that photos produced to prove he'd reached the summit of Mount McKinley had been faked. So his claim to have reached the top was also likely to have been untrue.

However, Cook had friends too. He was backed by the *New York Times*'s major rival, the *New York Herald*. He stuck to his story about his records, claiming he would have them returned to America as soon as possible. He dismissed Ahwelah and Etukishook's allegations by claiming his simple Inuit companions had been frightened of straying from land. To soothe their fears, he'd often pointed to low-lying clouds on the horizon, telling them it was land. This was quite plausible. It wasn't uncommon for seafarers to mistake banks of low clouds for distant land.

The *New York Times* and *Herald* slugged it out on behalf of their respective champions. The western world was fascinated by this rather comical dispute. British magazine *Punch* printed a cartoon showing the Cook and Peary waxworks at Madame Tussaud's punching each other, while British explorer Ernest Shackleton looks on in amazement. To begin with, public opinion was behind Cook. Despite his flimsy evidence, he was so much more likeable than Peary. But, over the next few months, Cook's case crumbled – especially when his navigation records failed to appear. His awards were withdrawn. Sensing defeat, he vanished, reportedly seen in London, Santiago and his home ground, Brooklyn.

Peary had won. The *National Geographic Society* pronounced him the first man to reach the Pole. The US government awarded him the rank of rear admiral, and he retired with a handsome pension. Yet his fame and acclaim never brought him any great happiness. His own records, scrutinized closely during the controversy with Cook, offered far from certain proof that he'd actually reached the Pole himself. Britain's *Royal Geographical Society*, while hailing him as a great explorer, always hedged their bets when it came to recognizing him as the first man to reach the Pole.

A blood disease (which he'd first been diagnosed as having by none other than Frederick Cook, after an earlier expedition) came back to claim him.

Peary died on February 20, 1920. He was 64.

Cook's fate was more tragic still. He became entangled in a fraud case about land, and was sent to prison. He died in 1940, still proclaiming he really had been to the North Pole.

Nearly a century later, modern polar historians are still asking if *either* of them actually reached the Pole. Cook's own case was pretty much destroyed in the year after he presented it. But Peary's extraordinary speed across the ice on his return journey also seems too good to be true. He kept careless navigational records, and his lack of what were considered to be reliable witnesses undermined his case in the eyes of his fellow explorers.

Millions of words have been written on what one writer called 'the dispute of the century'. Now it seems unlikely that either of them actually reached the Pole, even if Peary probably got considerably closer than Cook.

CHAPTER 5

AMUNDSEN'S HOLLOW VICTORY

American sports coach 'Red' Saunders once said: "Winning isn't everything. It's the only thing." Saunders had obviously never heard of Roald Amundsen. This tremendously capable Norwegian explorer became the first man to lead a team to the South Pole, beating a rival British team, led by Robert Falcon Scott, by a month or more. Amundsen showed that careful planning and good sense could take five men to the most remote spot on earth with relative ease. Scott's expedition, by contrast, ended in tragedy, his poor planning and misjudgment leading to his own death, and that of four other men. Yet although Amundsen won the race to the Pole and brought his team home alive, it was Scott who would be celebrated as the greater hero.

As a boy, Amundsen had read about the exploits of Sir John Franklin. His hero was fellow Norwegian, Fridtjof Nansen, a world-famous Arctic pioneer. Amundsen made his first polar trip in 1898, at the age of 25. He'd been aboard the *Belgica*, on the Belgian-led expedition to Antarctica, which had also included Dr. Frederick Cook. The expedition ship was trapped in pack ice and forced to wait out the long polar winter. While some men went insane in the endless dark, and the crew fell to squabbling and scurvy, Amundsen thrived on the hardship. One officer recalled how he was, 'the biggest, the strongest, the bravest, and generally the best-dressed man for sudden emergencies.'

Amundsen's lifelong ambition had been to be the first to reach the North Pole. In 1910, he'd borrowed the Norwegian vessel, the *Fram*, which had been used by Nansen on his voyage. Amundsen was all set to sail north when he heard that Cook and Peary were both claiming they'd already reached it. Others would have been crushed by the disappointment, but within minutes of hearing the news, he simply changed his destination. He would sail south for the Antarctic instead.

In his quest for fame, Amundsen knew he would have to be cunning. The funds to finance his expedition (from the Norwegian government and private backers) had been for an Arctic trip. Perhaps they would withdraw if they knew they were now paying for an Antarctic expedition instead.

Amundsen also knew that British explorer Robert Falcon Scott was preparing for an assault on the South Pole. Any delay might rob him of the chance of beating Scott.

So, Amundsen didn't even tell his crew of his change of plan. Some of them must have been puzzled when parts for a base hut were brought on board, along with teams of dogs. Huts were only put up on land, and there was no land at the North Pole, only frozen sea. For Arctic expeditions, dogs were usually picked up nearer the destination.

The *Fram* slipped away from Norway on August 9, 1910, with a crew of 19 men. Only when they reached Madeira, off the coast of Morocco, were the men told their true destination. Most of them had probably guessed by then, given that the ship was going south and the weather was getting warmer. Here, Amundsen also notified the Norwegian government, calculating that revealing his plans when he was already well into his journey would prevent them from stopping him.

Amundsen's knowledge of polar travel had led him to believe that the best way to travel was with skis, and sleds pulled by dogs – a method perfected by the Arctic inhabitants. He knew his rival, Scott, intended to use Manchurian ponies as well as dogs, and to have his men haul sleds, which was a less effective method, in Amundsen's eyes. The British were also taking three motorized sleds which troubled Amundsen. If the motorized sleds were a success, then there was every chance Scott would reach the Pole before the Norwegians.

The *Fram* sailed to Antarctica through the Ross Sea, taking only a week to negotiate the pack ice. The crew unloaded their equipment in the Bay of Whales, naming their camp Framheim ('*Fram*'s home'). They immediately began preparing for the trek south, making themselves comfortable for the coming winter. The plan was to lay down supply dumps at intervals along the route. This was to ensure that the party that went to the Pole would always have enough fuel and food. When they had done this, they would settle down to wait until the Antarctic spring – September to October – when they would make the dash for the Pole.

The Norwegians adapted very easily to polar conditions, perhaps because they came from a country well-used to snow and cold, and long, dark nights. They worked through blizzards, laying down three supply dumps as planned. When the winter weather forced a stop to the preparations, they retired to the hut. It was uncomfortably crowded, so they built a warren of underground corridors and chambers next to it, hewn from the snow and ice that soon built up around them. There were workshops, a place to cook, a room for the cook's slops, a lavatory, and even a stove-powered sauna. In their underground warren, they prepared for the trip, shaving the wood on their sleds to remove any unnecessary weight, until all the sleds were a third lighter.

Fearing the British would beat them, the Norwegians began their southward trek at the beginning of September. But it was too soon. The weather proved too harsh, and Amundsen and his men were forced to return, suffering from frostbite and exhaustion.

This time, they waited more patiently for the weather to turn warmer. By October 20, conditions were judged to be right, and they set off once again. Along with Amundsen were Olav Bjaarland, Helmer Hanssen, Sverre Hassel and Oskar Wisting, plus 52 dogs pulling four sleds. Their supplies had been meticulously packed over the winter. The men didn't ride the sleds, as it would have created unnecessary weight for the dogs to pull, but ran or skied alongside them. Every sled was pulled by a team of dogs in a fan formation, each dog having its own leash and harness, so that if it fell into a crevasse it wouldn't drag any of the others with it.

Amundsen planned to cover 24km (15 miles) a day. He could have gone faster, but didn't want to exhaust the dogs. Right from this second start, luck was with them. By November 4, they had reached the last of the supply dumps laid down in the autumn. From here Amundsen decided to set up a new dump every 112km (70 miles) – roughly four days travel – on the way to the Pole. This way, they would have less to carry with them on their return journey. These dumps were clearly marked by a flag on a stick, and a series of smaller pennants, placed on either side. The markers would direct them back to the dump if they became lost in a blizzard.

Each night, the men set up their tents and slept comfortably in sleeping bags made of three layers of fur. At the top of the Axel Heiberg Glacier, half the dogs were shot. With supplies left behind in a trail of dumps, they were simply not needed to pull the sleds any more. Their bodies were fed to both the other dogs and the explorers. There were now 18 dogs left, to pull three sleds in teams of six.

It wasn't all plain sailing, though. As they neared the Pole, the sleds had to cross a terrifying stretch of ice the men named the Devil's Glacier. Crevasses stretched in every direction, often hidden by snow, promising a violent death to anyone unlucky enough to plunge into their hidden depths. Hassel and Amundsen, roped together, gingerly probed forward, painstakingly charting a safe route through. Right after this obstacle, there was a vast plain of thin ice which they called the Devil's

Ballroom. Here, the surface was often too weak to support a man's weight, and it was all too easy to plummet down through the ice into a deep crack.

Taking regular sightings with a navigational instrument called a sextant, they edged toward their goal. Finally, at three in the afternoon, on December 14, 1911, Amundsen came forward to be the first to stand on a spot they took to be the very bottom of the world. They set up a tent and marked it with their national flag. Inside the tent, Amundsen left a letter for the Norwegian monarch, King Haakon VII. With it was a note for Scott, asking him to deliver it. Ever practical, Amundsen feared his party might not survive their return journey, and he wanted the world to know he had made it to the Pole first.

The men celebrated their victory with a feast of seal meat saved especially for the occasion. After spending two days taking readings to ensure they were exactly where they thought they were, they set off for home. The weather was not as good as it had been on the way out, but they still made good progress.

Back at Framheim base, the men waiting for them were unexpectedly roused by a knock on the window. It was four in the morning, January 26, 1912. Amundsen and his team had made 2,993km (1,860 miles) in 99 days. Coffee was swiftly brewed. Strangely enough, it was a full hour before anyone got around to asking whether or not Amundsen had actually made it to the Pole.

The *Fram* sailed soon after, arriving at Hobart, Tasmania, on March 7. News of Amundsen's success was telegraphed across the world. But Norway's polar heroes were soon to have their achievement eclipsed by a glorious failure.

CHAPTER 6

THE NOBLE ART OF DYING LIKE A GENTLEMAN

From the earliest days of Antarctic exploration, the British behaved as if it were their right to reach the South Pole first. After all, so much of the world was theirs anyway. The president of the *Royal Geographical Society*, Sir Clements Markham, appointed Royal Navy officer Robert Falcon Scott to lead a team to claim the Pole.

Scott, fated to become one of the most famous polar explorers ever, was a complex and not entirely likeable man. An unapologetic snob, given to black moods, he was driven by a strong sense of duty and patriotism. A whiff of his haughty character can be gained from this diary entry, describing his expedition deputy Teddy Evans as: "a thoroughly well-meaning little man but rather a duffer in anything but his own peculiar work."

Scott had first been to Antarctica in 1901. He'd set out to explore the interior, but scurvy had undermined his expedition. With him on that trip was Ernest Shackleton (see chapter 7). Both strong characters, the two men fell out, and became rivals. Another passenger was Dr. Edward Wilson, a keen birdwatcher and a talented artist. He'd recently suffered from the lung disease, tuberculosis, but this didn't stop him from wanting to explore the most hostile region on earth. He and Scott forged a friendship that would endure until their deaths.

Heavily influenced by his mentor, Sir Clements, Scott had a romantic view of polar exploration. It involved heroic, determined men hauling heavy sleds through ice and snow, and triumphing against frightening odds. This approach meant other more practical alternatives were not fully taken up. Few of the British party ever really learned to ski, for example.

Arctic inhabitants used dogs to pull their sleds, but men like Scott saw dogs as loyal companions. Using them as beasts of burden, driving them to exhaustion and then killing them for food when they were no longer needed, was unthinkable. Scott did use dogs in the end, but he never employed them with the same ruthlessness as his rivals.

By 1910, Scott and Shackleton had both led expeditions to the Antarctic. The Germans, Swedes and French had also explored the edges of the continent. Scott began to plan and recruit for his trip as the decade drew to a close. A meeting with the great Fridjof Nansen (see page 35) convinced him to review some of his prejudices. This time, they would take skis with them and they'd also use animals. The sleds would be towed by Manchurian ponies, but they would also take a small team of dogs. Scott still preferred ponies over dogs, despite the fact that Shackleton had found them unsuitable for polar conditions on his 1907 expedition.

Over 8,000 men volunteered for the expedition. By the summer of 1910, Scott had funds, a ship named the *Terra Nova*, and a crew of 67. Among them were his friend, Dr. Wilson, and another veteran from the 1901 expedition, Edgar 'Taff' Evans. Scott greatly admired this energetic Welshman, whose inventiveness and good nature made him an ideal companion.

Also among the crew were two men who'd made their careers in India. Perhaps they felt the Antarctic would make a refreshing change from India's sultry heat. Captain Lawrence 'Titus' Oates was a cavalry officer, whose job was to look after the ponies. He seemed to have little idea of what he was letting himself in for, describing the

Antarctic climate in a letter to his mother as: 'healthy but inclined to be cold'. Lieutenant Henry 'Birdy' Bowers was a Royal Indian Marine officer. He too had never been to the Antarctic, but he'd read a great deal about it.

The *Terra Nova* sailed from Cardiff on June 15, 1910. With the crew were 19 ponies, 33 dogs and three motor sleds. Scott hoped that the sleds – very modern and very expensive – would make setting up camps on the way to the Pole much easier. The welfare of the ponies, meanwhile, locked up as they were in cramped stables on the ship for the duration of the voyage, caused him constant worry.

The *Terra Nova* reached Melbourne, Australia, on October 13. Here, Scott discovered that Amundsen was also on his way to the Pole. From this moment, Scott knew he was in a race. When Wilson learned of Amundsen's parallel attempt, he wrote in his diary: "He will probably reach the Pole this year, earlier than we can, for not only will he travel much faster with dogs and expert ski runners than we shall with ponies, but he will be able to start earlier than we can, as we don't want to expose the ponies to any October temperatures."

They sailed for Antarctica via New Zealand, where Taff Evans disgraced himself. Despite all his great qualities, Evans liked a drink. On their final stopover, he got so drunk that he fell off the ship. Much to the relief of many of Scott's officers, who had looked down their noses at him, Evans was fired. Nevertheless, he managed to talk Scott into letting him back on board, little suspecting what fate had in store for him.

It took the *Terra Nova* three weeks to make it through the pack ice. (Amundsen's *Fram* had done it in a week.) They reached McMurdo Sound on January 2, 1911, and unloaded the cargo at Cape Evans. Almost at once, disaster struck. When one of the motor sleds was taken off the ship, it broke through the ice and sank like a stone.

Meanwhile, over in the Bay of Whales, 650km (400 miles) to the east, Amundsen was laying down food and fuel depots in a line heading from his base camp, toward the Pole…

As the polar summer turned to autumn, Scott's team discovered that Shackleton had been right about the ponies. They were a poor choice. On one exploratory trip, seven out of eight ponies died. Ponies needed a lot of looking after, and had to eat hay. Dogs were less fussy, and would even eat each other if necessary. The dogs were also faster, and adapted to the freezing conditions more easily. That said, Scott and his men were never able to train their dogs as well as their Norwegian rivals did.

Winter brought an end to the laying of depots. Scott had intended to set down fuel and food a month or so away from the Pole, in a place they called One Ton Depot, but the ponies found it such a struggle that the men had to settle for a spot 50km (30 miles) further north. As the expedition drew to its tragic end, this distance would prove to be vital.

The Antarctic winter passed and spring came.

On October 24, 1911, Scott began his bid for the Pole. Over in the Bay of Whales, Amundsen had left four days earlier – and he had also chosen a starting point that was closer to the Pole.

There were problems right from the start. The motor sleds, on which Scott had spent so much of his budget, set out first. They were supposed to lay down supplies along the route, but they lasted just five days, their engines unable to cope with the extreme cold. Scott himself set off with his main party on November 1. The ponies struggled, sinking into the snow and suffering terribly. By December 9, they'd had to shoot them all. The dogs were a greater success, but Scott was still uncomfortable with the idea of using them, and sent them back to his base camp on December 11.

Scott spent time on his journey exploring and making maps, which made his progress slower. As Amundsen neared the Pole, Scott's team were still manhauling heavy sleds up the Beardmore Glacier. When Scott's team reached the top, four men returned to Cape Evans, leaving eight to press on in two teams of four. As they neared the Pole, Scott chose a team of just four to make the final push. This would make the most of their limited supplies.

In 1911, radio technology was still very new. The idea of carrying a radio set to the Pole to keep in touch with events was unthinkable. This meant Scott's team couldn't follow Amundsen's progress. Unknown to them – or anyone else – Amundsen had reached the Pole on December 14. While Scott was still choosing who to take with him, Amundsen was already on his way back to his base camp.

Scott chose Evans, Oates, Wilson and 'Birdy' Bowers – so-called because of his big, beaky nose. So intense were the men's ambitions to reach the Pole that one of the men not selected, a tough Irish sailor named Thomas Crean, wept when he was told.

With hindsight, Scott's decision to take four men with him was one of his greatest mistakes, although he had good reasons. Hauling the sleds would be easier with five men than four and, at the time, food supplies looked plentiful. On the other hand, everything on the trip had been made for only four people. The tents were for four, and the sleds carried rations for four, the supply dumps for the return journey were equipped for four.

There was another problem, too. Evans had a festering wound on his hand. He'd concealed this from Scott – perhaps from sheer pluck and determination, or possibly fear that it would disqualify him from being in the final party. Oates too was suffering from an old war wound, although this was common knowledge.

Amundsen had had great good luck on his polar trek, but not Scott. As his team trudged on to the Pole, fate began to conspire against them.

On January 16, a few miles short of their goal, they spotted a black flag in the snow. It was one of Amundsen's food store markers. This could only mean one thing – the Norwegians had reached the Pole first. They arrived at the Pole the next day, to be confronted by the Norwegians' silk tent. Hopeful that Amundsen might have calculated its position wrongly, they made a thorough check with their navigational instruments. But it soon dawned on them that Amundsen had found the exact spot.

Scott was deeply offended by the note left by Amundsen, asking him to deliver a letter to the Norwegian king. Perhaps it didn't occur to Scott that the Norwegians feared for their own return.

The five men then took the customary team photographs – among the saddest images from this great era of exploration. Scott and his men pose as if for a school sports photo. Evans and Oates sit cross-legged at the front, with Bowers, Scott and Wilson standing behind them. Scott, the team captain, is in the middle. The men's disappointment is pitifully obvious. Their bodies slump, their hands hang at their sides, and they stare into the camera with glum faces, like resentful boys forced out on a rainy picnic. What these photos cannot convey is the cold. As the men posed for their polar pictures, a sharp, damp wind would have crept through their clothing and chilled them to the marrow.

Scott's journal of that day makes plain his disappointment. "Great God! This is an awful place," he wrote. Not only was he distressed not to have been the first to reach the Pole, he was also beginning to worry whether they'd get back alive.

Scott was right to worry. He already had frostbite. The weather was much colder than they'd expected. They were one man more than their dwindling food and fuel supplies were intended for. Scurvy was beginning to weaken them. As a final twist, the fuel containers they'd left at supply depots were now showing a worrying tendency to leak in the freezing temperatures.

Scott's progress had been slow, but the party still paused to spend half a day collecting rock samples on the Beardmore Glacier. Time lost here would prove precious later in the journey. Still, the samples gathered were of great scientific interest, providing the first clues that Antarctica had once been covered with forests. The fossilized ferns they collected were very similar to ferns found in South Africa, South America, India and Australia, offering proof that Antarctica had once been part of a 'supercontinent' made up of all the countries in the southern half of the world.

On February 3, Evans and Scott both fell into one of Antarctica's icy crevasses. Roped to their heavy sled, they didn't fall far, but later that day, Evans started behaving oddly. He became, 'rather stupid and incapable', as Scott recorded sternly in his diary. Over the next few days, his health deteriorated dramatically.

By February 16, Evans had become giddy and sick. His ski boots kept falling off his feet, and he was forever lagging behind the others. He'd been slowly worn to a frazzle by his festering hand-wound and now the shock of the fall. As they trudged through the snow, he finally collapsed. His companions found him kneeling, his clothing muddled, his speech slurred, and his eyes wild with fear and confusion. They picked him up, but he fell into a coma, and died soon after midnight the next day. The party was back to four.

By now, they were all suffering from severe frostbite, but Oates was the worst affected. His feet were so badly swollen, he had to slit his snow boots to get them on, which did nothing for the boots' ability to keep out the cold and damp. He suggested several times that his friends leave him behind, as he was obviously holding them up, but they wouldn't abandon him. So, one morning, after they'd made camp, Oates stood up and announced: "I am just going outside and may be some time." No one stopped him as he stumbled into the blizzard outside the tent. Then there were three.

At this point, Scott made some alarming calculations. They were 88km (55 miles) from One Ton Depot, where there was enough food and fuel to ensure their survival. They currently had supplies for another seven days. In their crippled condition they could cover no more than 10km (6 miles) a day. At this rate, at the end of seven days, they'd still be 21km (13 miles) from the depot. The sum added up to almost certain death. "I doubt if we can possibly do it," Scott wrote. But, he reasoned, with Oates no longer holding them up, they might still have a chance. Maybe they would have had, if the weather hadn't worsened.

On March 21, two months after the crushing disappointment of finding that Amundsen had beaten them to the Pole, Scott and his two remaining companions set up their final camp. They were just 18km (11 miles) from One Ton Depot. By now, Scott's frostbite had turned to gangrene. "Amputation is the least I can hope for," he wrote in his diary. Their luck was not about to turn. There was talk of Bowers, the strongest of the three, making a go of reaching One Ton Depot to bring back food and fuel, but the blizzard that raged outside their tent blew full and furious for the next ten days. It was the final straw.

Scott was a haughty, arrogant man, but in his final days, with the prospect of death utterly certain, his dignified acceptance of his fate was deeply moving. They all knew they were going to die. All they could do was wait for nature to take its course.

In their tent, the 43-year-old Scott wrote to his family, colleagues and friends, and penned comforting words to the wives and mothers of his companions. To the expedition backers, he wrote: "We have been to the Pole and we shall die like gentlemen." To his wife Kathleen Scott he wrote: "I had looked forward to helping you bring [our son] up... Make the boy interested in natural history if you can. It is better than games." (She succeeded. Their son, Peter Scott, became a famous wildlife artist and conservationist.)

Finally, fully aware of the great interest his death would spark in the world, he wrote a final 'Message To The Public'. It concluded, "Had we lived, I should have had a tale to tell of the hardihood, endurance, and courage of my companions which would have stirred the heart of every Englishman. These rough notes and our dead bodies must tell the tale…"

He finished his journal with the words: "It seems a pity but I do not think I can write more – R. Scott." The handwriting looks calm, almost unhurried, as if he were writing a leisurely postcard. However, there is one final, brief entry underneath, scrawled with little attention to punctuation. This last entry ends with what sounds like a desperate plea: 'look after our people'.

It's all too easy to imagine Scott starving and shivering to death in his sleeping bag, tormented by his gangrenous foot and by his failure, full of remorse for the men who were dying with him and the family he would leave behind. Perhaps, days later, he roused himself to add that final message with clumsy, freezing fingers.

Over the weeks that followed, the tent was half-covered by successive snow storms. Its tip was eventually spotted eight months later, on

November 12, by a search team from the *Terra Nova* who had had far better luck with the weather. Edward Atkinson, the expedition surgeon, was the first to enter. Preserved by the extreme cold, Bowers and Wilson looked as if they were sleeping peacefully. Scott, his face contorted, was twisted half-out of his sleeping bag. His had evidently not been an easy end. His diary lay beneath his shoulders. Something everyone noted about the interior was how tidy it was. Clearly Scott's regime of ship-shape neatness had been kept up to the end.

The tent had an outer and inner layer. The search team removed the outer layer and took it with them, along with the men's journals, letters, photographic plates and rock samples. The inner layer they let fall over the three dead men, and a pile of stones, topped by a cross made of skis, was built over the spot. Of Oates there was no sign, although his sleeping bag was found.

The expedition was expected back in New Zealand in April 1913. Like the rest of the world,

Kathleen Scott didn't know what had happened to her husband, and set out from England in January to meet him. Scott's expedition ship *Terra Nova* carried no radio, so the crew was only able to pass on the news when they returned to New Zealand. Kathleen Scott was aboard a ship in the Pacific when a telegraph came through on February 19, informing her of Scott's death.

In Britain, the news was greeted with widespread disappointment and led to huge public displays of grief. The outer layer of Scott's tent was erected at the Earl's Court Exhibition Centre in London, and thousands filed silently past this canvas shrine.

Reports that Scott's expedition was £30,000 in debt led to many generous donations, which eventually raised £75,500. After the expenses had been paid, wages settled and funds provided for relatives, there was enough left over to form the Scott Polar Research Institute in Cambridge. There is a small public museum there now, containing, among other items, Oates's sleeping bag.

The tragedy robbed Amundsen of his victory. Overshadowed by the noble heroism of Scott's end, the Norwegian was often ridiculed. When Amundsen was at a dinner given by Britain's *Royal Geographical Society*, then the most prestigious scientific and exploratory organization in the world, a toast was proposed, not to Amundsen, but to the dogs who had pulled him to the Pole. The British, in their pride, could not forgive the Norwegians for reaching the Pole first – and with dogs. It seemed to them to be, in a phrase popular at the time, 'unsporting'.

CHAPTER 7

"WHAT THE ICE GETS, THE ICE KEEPS"

Frank Worsley lay on his hotel bed, sleeping the restless slumber of a deep-water sailor away from the sea. He was in London on shore leave. It was the summer of 1914 and, all around, there was talk of war. Worsley, a born adventurer from New Zealand, who had been at sea since he was 16, sensed interesting times ahead.

As he drifted through the night, a strange dream disturbed his sleep. He was at the wheel of a sailing ship, but the boat was not at sea. It was edging down Burlington Street, off London's Regent Street. All around were huge, glacial ice-blocks.

The next morning, he hurried down to Burlington Street. There, a sign on a door reading 'Imperial Trans-Antarctic Expedition' caught his eye, and Worsley was drawn inside. The first person he saw was Sir Ernest Shackleton, a famous polar explorer. Shackleton had been to the Antarctic twice before, with Robert Falcon Scott in 1901, and as leader of his own expedition over 1907-1909. With both Poles 'conquered', he was planning one last, epic trip – the crossing of the entire Antarctic continent. It was a venture Shackleton described as, 'the largest and most striking of all journeys'.

The two struck up an instant understanding. "The moment I set eyes on him," Worsley recalled, "I knew that he was a man with whom I should be proud to work." Shackleton, who hired his crews on gut instinct, knew at once that Worsley was his sort of fellow. Worsley was taken on as captain of Shackleton's expedition vessel, the *Endurance*.

Fifteen months later, the two men and their crew were stranded on an ice floe, as *Endurance* was about to sink through the ice into the freezing waters of the Weddell Sea. They were hundreds of miles from anyone, totally without hope of rescue in the most pitiless place on earth. Shackleton turned to Worsley and said wistfully, "Perhaps it's a pity, skipper, that you dreamed a dream that sent you to Burlington Street that morning we met."

Worsley replied, with no hesitation, "No, I've never regretted it, and never shall, even if we don't get through."

Shackleton had that effect on his people – he inspired a deep, fierce loyalty. In the terrible situation they were now in, he'd need every ounce of his forceful character to hold his team together.

The Imperial Trans-Antarctic Expedition had set sail from London in August 1914 – the very month the First World War broke out. On hearing the news, Shackleton immediately offered to make his ship and crew available for the war, but received a one word reply from the British Admiralty: 'Proceed'. So the *Endurance* sailed away, leaving a sedate, elegant world of blooming prosperity, straw hats, brass bands and seaside promenades, which the coming war would change forever.

Aboard the ship were 29 men – a hand-picked selection of officers, seamen, scientists and craftsmen, as well as a photographer and artist. The ship's carpenter, an irascible Scot named 'Chippy' McNeish, also brought his cat, known to everyone as Mrs. Chippy.

Shackleton's plan was a bold one. There had been much to learn from recent polar successes and failures. He intended to cross the South Pole using a team of nearly 70 sled dogs to haul a six-man party over the bottom of the world. The team would set out from the Weddell Sea and head for the Ross Ice Shelf and Ross Sea. Here, another ship, the *Aurora*, would be waiting to ferry them home. As they set out from the west, a team from the *Aurora* was to lay down a series of depots on the route back to the Ross Sea – places for the sled team to refill their supplies and rest on the way back to safety.

Shackleton fitted his chosen role of professional explorer perfectly. He radiated great determination and sense of purpose. The Shackleton family motto was, 'By endurance we conquer', and he did everything to live up to it. Of medium build, but solid, he had a handsome, brooding face, with a square, forceful jaw. A manly character through and through, when first shown his newborn son, Raymond, he remarked that the baby had, 'good fists for fighting'. He had a generous nature too, and a wry wit. When presented with stowaway Pierce Blackboro, who had sneaked aboard the *Endurance* in Buenos Aires, he growled, "If we run out of food and anyone has to be eaten, you'll be the first."

Exploring was his passion. "You cannot imagine what it is like to walk in places where no man has walked before," he once told his sister. He said too, "Sometimes I think I'm no good at anything, except being away in the wilds." It was a reckless way of life that would cost him and his family dear.

By the time the *Endurance* reached the Antarctic island of South Georgia, it was November. Here, the ramshackle whaling station at Grytviken, where the bodies of whales were stripped of their oil and blubber, provided a last glimpse of human civilization. The news there was that the Weddell Sea was heavy with ice, so a route through to Antarctica would not be easy. Shackleton hesitated. This was not good, but, if he turned back, he might never have the chance to go again. He was now 40 years old, and his health was not improving. He had staked everything he had on this trip. Driven by the belief that this would be his last chance for glory, he set out from Grytviken on December 5, at the height of the polar summer. If the ice was bad now, it was not going to get any better.

While the *Endurance* sailed south, the crew was treated to a fantastic display of the Antarctic at its kindest and most brilliant. As the ship forged a route through the half-frozen sea, they passed huge, gleaming icebergs, cut by the wind and waves into fantastic, towering sculptures. The perpetual daylight of the polar summer often cast a beautiful pink glow over these bergs and ice floes.

The sea bubbled and teamed with life. Huge whales, some twice the length of the ship, would pass by, their blowholes spouting fountains of steam. As albatross and petrels circled above, lazy seals basking on the ice floes would raise a sleepy head to watch them pass. When the seals were not to be seen, penguins (the seals' main prey) would slither and waddle across the ice, croaking out to the ship as it passed. Best of all was the strange phenomenon of the ice shower, when moisture in the air would freeze into ice crystals and float slowly down in a sparkling, magical haze.

However, as Christmas approached, it became obvious that the *Endurance* was making very slow progress. On January 18, 1915, only 48km (30 miles) from the coast, ice closed in around the ship. In a single night the temperature dropped by 40°C (72°F). The crew was about to see a very different side of the Antarctic. They attacked the ice that surrounded the ship with picks, shovels and saws, but it soon became clear that the *Endurance* was stuck solid. It was, "like an almond in the middle of a chocolate bar," as one member of the crew put it.

The days were changing, too. Night fell for brief but lengthening periods, and the once plentiful seals and birds that surrounded the ship were now infrequent visitors. Their animal instincts were telling them this frozen world would soon be impossible to survive in, and they were heading north to warmer waters. The *Endurance*'s crew could only stay and prepare for whatever the polar winter could throw at them.

They were so close to land that the coast could sometimes even be seen from the ship. In clear water, it would have taken less than a day to reach. Shackleton never made his frustrations known. His job was to lead his men, and he did this by projecting an unshakable optimism. He knew that the coming winter was going to be very difficult, but he'd prepared for it well. Ever mindful of the fate of the crew of the *Belgica* (see page 36), he was determined to keep his men in good spirits.

There was a large library on the *Endurance* and the men had a well-ordered routine to keep the ship in good condition. They held football matches and dog sled races, and began to forge close working relationships with their dogs. Many built elaborate ice kennels for them, and puppies were born, much to everyone's delight. In the evening there were gramophone concerts, or the men would all sing along as meteorologist Leonard Hussey played the banjo.

Shackleton had seen how Scott had bred resentment among his men with his haughty style of leadership. In contrast, Shackleton worked side-by-side with his crew, and left no one in any doubt that their lives, rather than the ambitions of his expedition, were his most important concern.

On the darkest day of the polar winter, June 22, there was not a fleck of light in the sky. They had been stuck for over six months. Shackleton declared it a day of celebration. The ship's mess was decorated with flags and bunting, a stage was constructed and many of the crew came forward to perform. Appearing dressed up as a Methodist minister, a crazy professor and a female flamenco dancer, the men drank and sang their way through the night. Officer Lionel Greenstreet recorded in his diary: "We laughed until the tears ran down our cheeks." These, clearly, were men determined not to let their alarming circumstances get them down.

The ship's crew might have been in good spirits, but the *Endurance* itself was in a bad way. The ship had been built of greenheart – an especially tough wood – but even this was not strong enough to withstand the crushing pressure of thousands of tons of pack ice pressing around the hull. This was now building up so much that the ship was being squeezed to destruction.

Some polar ships had been built with hulls designed to rise above crushing pack ice, but not the *Endurance*. Deck planks began to split with sudden, ferocious cracks like gunshots. Again, the men tried to dig the ice away from the hull to ease the pressure, but it was an endless, pointless task.

Eventually, Shackleton confided in Worsley, "The ship can't live like this, skipper. It's only a matter of time. What the ice gets, the ice keeps."

By the end of October, the *Endurance* had ceased to be a safe place to live, and the order was given to abandon ship. Supplies, sleds, three lifeboats, the dogs, puppies and ship's cat, were all bundled overboard. Tents were set up on the ice. Shackleton announced that they would draw lots to divide up the sleeping bags. There were both wool and fur sleeping bags, but the fur ones were much warmer. The draw was fixed. All the officers got the wool ones – the men got fur.

There were still difficult decisions to be made, though, and there was little room for sentimentality. Shackleton decided that the puppies and the cat would have to be shot. This decision upset many of his men. In the robust, all-male world of the *Endurance*, these animals had provided an opportunity for the crew to show a softer side. On the journey over, the cat had fallen overboard, and the ship had turned around to rescue her from the Atlantic. This time, Mrs. Chippy was not so lucky.

With the ship creaking and groaning behind him, like a huge animal in its death throes, Shackleton called his men together. With no trace of drama or regret, he told them plainly that the *Endurance* could no longer carry them. So now they, and their dogs and sleds, were going home. Put so plainly, it sounded like a reasonable course of action, but the reality was very different. Hauling heavy sleds was hot, sweaty, exhausting work. They made such slow progress across the ice fields that, even after three days, they could still see their ship.

Shackleton had a talent for constantly reworking his plans. Heading for safety across the frozen sea was clearly not going to work. So they returned to the ship – now a frozen, eerie hulk, its once-snug interior covered with ice – and rescued many of the supplies they'd left behind. Expedition photographer Frank Hurley had left many beautiful photographic plates in the ship. Known as glass-plate negatives, these heavy, pane-of-glass sized images produced much better photographs than the recently invented photographic film. The decision was made to rescue this evidence of their ordeal, but when Hurley entered the *Endurance*, he found the area where he'd left the plates under four foot of ice and water. There was nothing to do but strip down to his underwear and dive in to get them.

On November 21, the broken, waterlogged ship finally sank. Surrounded by the wreckage of fallen masts and rigging, the bow slid down into the icy water and the stern rose high in the air. The heavy, steel bolts which anchored the *Endurance*'s powerful steam-engine in place were wrenched out. With a terrifying sound of splintering wood, the iron engine dropped through deck partitions into the now-vertical bow, dragging the ship down to the black bottom of the Weddell Sea. It was a heart-breaking moment. Shackleton wrote in his journal: "At 5:00pm she went down. I cannot write about it." For a brief while there was a small hole in the ice, but it soon closed. The *Endurance* was gone.

The crew settled uneasily into their new home on the ice. The frozen crust was five foot thick, and might have given the impression they were on solid ground. But seeing the ship go down was a sharp reminder that, below them, was a vast sea of freezing water. Still, Shackleton made every effort to keep his men cheerful, despite his own failing health. Soon after the *Endurance* sank, pains in his legs forced him to spend two weeks in his tent.

Another attempt to march north seemed to be the only thing left to do, but the ship's lifeboats each weighed at least a ton. They had to be hauled along by teams of men in harness – a difficult task over rough ice. As they tried to start their long journey home yet again, Shackleton was faced with open mutiny. Chippy McNeish, still bitter about the death of his cat, refused to haul the boats. He told Shackleton his duty to him was relinquished now that the ship had sunk.

Shackleton knew the only hope they had of getting back alive was to work together as a team. If McNeish was allowed to influence other resentful crew members, the party would split into warring factions, and they would all be doomed. Forceful action was required. McNeish was bluntly told he would be shot if he didn't obey orders.

Shackleton then called his men together. He reassured them that they would still be paid until they reached a safe port, and explained that it was essential for everyone to work together. Finally, he announced that the hauling would stop. It was too exhausting. They would simply have to drift north with the ice, as they had been doing when the *Endurance* was still afloat, and then take to the boats when the pack ice began to break up.

Shackleton may have seemed forceful and in command, but he was so shaken by McNeish's rebellion that he couldn't sleep the following night. There were difficult decisions to make, too. With the idea of sledding north abandoned, there was no sense in continuing to feed their teams of dogs. They had enough problems keeping themselves alive on the limited supply of seals and penguins they managed to catch. Shooting the dogs was heart-wrenching, but kinder than letting them loose to starve to death on the ice.

For four months, the men drifted. At night, they curled up in their sleeping bags and tried to summon up enough warmth to sleep. They ate a monotonous diet of seal meat, supplemented by their dwindling food supplies, and prayed that they would soon reach the open sea. In early April, just as the polar summer was drawing to an end, the ice they stood on began to move with the swell of the ocean. Men began to feel seasick, but this could only mean they were nearing open water.

On April 9, the boats were readied and set out to sea. After 14 months stranded on the ice, they were finally free – but free to do what?

The journey that followed was seven days of freezing, wet torment. A hundred and fifty miles to the north lay Snow Hill Island. Although the island was uninhabited, they knew supplies had been left there to help shipwrecked mariners. So it was there they set their sights. By day, they pushed on through towering seas, while the men who weren't rowing furiously bailed out water to keep their open boats afloat. By night, they clambered aboard passing ice floes, to shiver in their tents.

One night there was a loud crack, and the ice split through the middle of a tent. One of the crew fell through. He floundered in the freezing sea, trapped in his soaking sleeping bag, stunned by the shock of the icy water. Shackleton ran over, thrust a hand into the gap, and pulled the man out, bag and all. An instant later, the split closed up with a crash. From then on, the men slept in the boats.

Perhaps it was the thought that they were actually doing something, rather than just drifting, that kept the crew going. Their hands were so cold that they had to be chipped off the oars at the end of a shift. Dysentery – a serious stomach complaint – swept through the boats, and everyone suffered from a raging thirst and hunger.

Now, at night, the three boats were roped together to prevent them from drifting apart. But, as men tried to sleep, they would be disturbed by killer whales, blowing air through their blowholes, 'like suddenly escaping steam'. The whales brushed against the boats, threatening to sever the ropes that held them together. Occasionally they would peer out of the water, presenting the crew with a dark open mouth and sharp, white, gleaming teeth. The threat of death hung in the air and men wept in despair. His boats swamped and his men nearly finished, Shackleton changed his plans again. If they kept on to Snow Hill Island, he knew they wouldn't all reach there alive. So they altered course for Elephant Island, which was nearer, but had no supplies.

On their seventh day at sea, the brooding cliffs of Elephant Island loomed before them. This barren slab of rock, ice and snow would have to make do as their new home. The boats forged ashore through swirling reefs and treacherous currents, and the men staggered onto the shingle beach, some delirious with joy. It was the first time any of them had stood on solid land for 497 days. They had had yet another close escape. One of Shackleton's men estimated that some of them would have died within a day if they hadn't landed on the island.

It had been impossible to cook at sea, but ashore hot drinks and food were prepared. Tents were set up, and the men could feel their strength returning. But Elephant Island was not a place where anyone would wish to stay, and the men soon grew to loathe it. Apart from elephant seals (from which the island took its name) and penguins, there was almost nothing there to eat. Constant sleet, snow and rain hammered down, and the rock was not on any known shipping route, so there was still no chance of rescue. So Shackleton did the only thing he could do. He prepared to set out to another island where he could get help.

There were several options open to him, all of which were extremely dangerous. The nearest inhabited land was near Cape Horn, on the tip of South America. But the wind blew constantly east on the route to the Cape, making it impossible to reach in a small boat coming from the opposite direction. An alternative destination was the island of South Georgia. It was from here that they had set off for the South Pole, in the faraway days of December, 1914. This, at least, was in the path of the wind – but it was 1,300km (800 miles) away, across one of the most dangerous oceans on earth.

Not all of them would go, of course. Shackleton decided six men would make the journey. Frank Worsley would come, and second officer Thomas

Crean, who had been with Scott on his final, fatal expedition. Shackleton also took a couple of men who were known troublemakers, including Chippy McNeish. For all his faults, McNeish was proving to be indispensable. He had a genius for improvisation. Such was his skill and confidence with wood that, when they were stranded, he had offered to build a smaller ship from the remains of the *Endurance*. Now he set to work on the biggest lifeboat, the *James Caird*, to make it as seaworthy as possible for the journey ahead. The sides, or gunnels, were raised with wood from packing cases, and bits and pieces from the other two boats were used to strengthen the hull. Oil paint and seal blood was used to make the new seams watertight.

Leaving the rest of the men behind with second-in-command, Frank Wild, the *James Caird* put to sea on April 24, 1916. Shackleton and his small crew watched the 21 men left behind wave them off until they were out of sight. Perhaps it was lucky they couldn't see that many of the men had tears streaming down their faces. Most of those on the shore were convinced they would never see the crew of the *James Caird* again.

The journey was every bit as dreadful as everyone expected. They set out in calm weather, but it soon turned stormy. Huge waves dwarfed the tiny boat, and freezing rain constantly hammered down on them. The six men took turns to row and steer and bail and sleep – four hours on, and four hours off – but there was not a single moment when they were not soaking and shivering. How they didn't freeze to death remains a mystery. Most extraordinary of all, navigator Frank Worsley was only able to take four sightings with his sextant in over two weeks at sea. For the rest of the time he steered by 'dead reckoning', a sailor's term meaning guesswork and instinct.

On the 14th day, seaweed floated past the boat – a sure sign that land was near. But, just as the cliffs of South Georgia began to peer over the horizon, a ferocious storm blew up. Again, Frank

Worsley was the hero of the hour. With extraordinary skill, he managed to steer the *James Caird* away from reefs and rocks that would have dashed the men to death. Elsewhere off South Georgia, the same storm claimed a 500-ton steamer.

On the evening of May 10, after 17 days at sea, they landed at King Haakon Bay on South Georgia. It was the wrong side of the island, 35km (22 miles) from Stromness, the nearest inhabited settlement, but it would have to do. After four days recovering from the trip, Shackleton, Worsley and Crean felt strong enough to set out for help. The boat, and the other three men, remained behind.

Between them and rescue lay a series of steep mountain peaks and glaciers – an uncharted island interior no one had ever crossed. Shackleton was not a man to let such details bother him. After McNeish had fitted screws to their boots, to act as crude crampons, Shackleton, Worsley and Crean set off under a luminous full moon.

The journey they made wouldn't be repeated for

another forty years, and only then by experienced and fully-equipped mountain climbers. The three men waded through snow, dodging glaciers and precipices, knowing that to stop would be to risk death from exposure. High on a ridge and tiring fast in an icy wind, Shackleton took a huge, devil-may-care risk. Certain they would freeze to death if they stayed much longer, he coiled his rope to make an improvised toboggan. All three sat on it, and shot down a steep snow slope to the valley below. They could have been dashed to pieces on sharp rocks, or fallen into a crevasse or over a cliff. But they didn't. Their luck held.

By daybreak, they were looking down on Fortuna Bay, near to Stromness, and rescue. At seven o'clock that morning, they heard the steam whistle that signalled the start of the morning shift at the whaling station. It was their first evidence of other human life for nearly a year and a half.

At three o'clock on the afternoon of May 20, 1916, three bedraggled, hairy men staggered into

Stromness. They were black from the soot of their blubber stoves, stinking abominably, their clothes in tatters – such a terrifying sight that children ran away from them screaming. Factory manager Thoralf Sörlle, who knew Shackleton well, was summoned to meet them.

"Who on earth are you?" he demanded.

One came forward and said, plainly, "My name is Ernest Shackleton."

Sörlle burst into tears. These men had come back from the dead.

The wait at Elephant Island had been dreadful. After the first month, each man would awake thinking today was the day they would be rescued. But days, weeks and months went by, and still no one came. By August, Frank Wild had reluctantly come to the conclusion that the *James Caird* had been lost. He began to plan another voyage away from their island prison. The truth, however, was more mundane. It took Shackleton three months and four attempts to get through the storms and ice, and back to Elephant Island. Eventually, he had to travel to Punta Arenas, in Chile, to obtain a boat equipped to make the journey.

On August 30, the men were preparing a meal of boiled seal backbone when a cry went up: "A ship!" Only then could anyone believe they would ever see their homes and families again. Shackleton was there on the rescue ship to greet them, barely able to speak. His ambitious journey had failed. No one, now, would cross the Antarctic until 1958. But his other ambition – to get every single member of his crew back to safety – had been achieved against extraordinary odds.

At Stromness, Shackleton had asked Sörlle when the war had ended.

"The war is not over," he had answered. "Millions are being killed. Europe is crazy. The world is crazy."

So the crew of the *Endurance* sailed back to a dreary, war-torn country, which was indifferent to their extraordinary ordeal. Heroes were dying

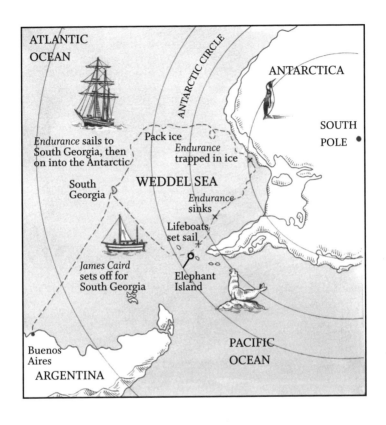

ATLANTIC
OCEAN

ANTARCTIC CIRCLE

ANTARCTICA

SOUTH
POLE

Endurance sails to
South Georgia, then
on into the Antarctic

Pack ice

Endurance
trapped in ice

South
Georgia

WEDDEL SEA

Endurance
sinks

Lifeboats
set sail

James Caird
sets off for
South Georgia

Elephant
Island

PACIFIC
OCEAN

Buenos
Aires

ARGENTINA

every day on the Western Front. Set against the
barbed wire, tanks and poison gas of the trenches,
adventurers like Shackleton were men out of time.

FROM 1916 TO THE PRESENT

Once almost impossibly remote, the Arctic and Antarctic are now easily accessible.

The North Pole can be reached by powerful icebreakers, by submarines and by ski planes. Weather stations drift across its frozen surface.

At the South Pole, there is a permanent settlement, the Scott-Amundsen Base, where huge C-130 transport planes land and take off when weather permits. The continent has 42 coastal and inland research stations.

However, despite this, the Poles have remained a challenge for adventurers. As the 20th century came to an end, explorers competed to reach or cross the Poles in the most dangerous, hair-raising ways. Where once whole teams of men would work together to reach a Pole, now they set out in ones or twos. At first, these attempts were 'supported', with supplies being dropped by plane, or left along the route by others. Once this had been achieved, people began to set new challenges, and some polar enthusiasts attempted to reach the Poles 'unsupported'.

Less than a century after the epic journeys of Amundsen, Peary, Shackleton and Scott, one man, with a sled full of supplies, can now cross over a on of the Poles entirely unaided. A Norwegian ex-commando named Børge Ousland did just that, when he crossed Antarctica in 2001. But even in the 21st century, exploring the polar regions can still be a nightmarish ordeal – as the next story shows…

CHAPTER 8

HARD TIMES AT THE BOTTOM OF THE WORLD

Ranulph Fiennes and Mike Stroud's 2,175km (1,350 mile) trek across the Antarctic had barely begun when Stroud fell into a crevasse. The two British adventurers were using parachute-like para-sails to haul them and their equipment across the Filchner Ice Shelf, on the opening stage of their journey.

It was Fiennes who first saw the dark blue jaws of the crevasse loom before them. He immediately threw himself to the ground, sliding to a bruising halt just before he reached its lip. Stroud was not so quick. As he fumbled with his sail-release cord, he heard Fiennes shout an anguished, "Noooooooo…," before the ground dropped away beneath him.

In a continent devoid of man-eating wildlife, crevasses offer the greatest threat of violent death. They're often hidden by a thin coating of snow, like a trap door. Anyone who stumbles onto one can end up plummeting into a dark, deep ice cavern.

Fortunately Stroud hadn't fallen far. He'd landed on a narrow platform of hardened snow, about twenty feet down, right next to his sled. On either side of him were vertical walls of ice. The bottom of the crevasse was too far below to see. Getting him out wouldn't be too difficult. The sled was another matter and, as it carried essential supplies, they had to retrieve it.

Every time Stroud moved, snow fell away from his precarious perch. When he tried to stand up, his foot went straight through the snow. By now, the shock of the fall was beginning to wear off, and he felt sick with fear. There was a long rope on the sled and Fiennes called down, telling him to throw it up to the surface. Stroud leaned over to reach for the sled, but it lurched away from him, and more snow and ice fell away. Eventually Stroud managed to get hold of the rope and throw it up to the top.

The only way to get the sled to the surface was to lighten its load, so Stroud lobbed up fuel bottles, food and other equipment, until the sled was empty. Only then could he climb up the crevasse. Once on top, he lay panting in the snow, haunted by his narrow brush with death.

Sir Ranulph Twisleton-Wykeham-Fiennes ('Ran' to his friends) and Dr. Mike Stroud were attempting the first unsupported crossing of the Antarctic. It was late November, 1992. In the months ahead of them, they hoped to walk, ski and sail to the South Pole, and then carry on to the Ross Sea. Stroud, 37, was a medical researcher specializing in nutrition, and a survival consultant for the Ministry of Defence. He planned to take records of the slow deterioration of their bodies as they battled against the hardships to come.

Fiennes, an ex-SAS army officer, educated at Eton, was an old-fashioned professional adventurer. At 48, he was beginning to wonder if he was too old for such expeditions – but, as he said at the time, "[This] is my job. It's the way I make my income." A veteran of many a hair-raising trek to the world's most dangerous locations, Fiennes made a living writing books and giving talks about his exploits. On this trip, the men also hoped to raise funds for research into the disease of multiple sclerosis. Every mile they walked would make huge sums of money from sponsors.

Fiennes and Stroud had been on polar expeditions together five times before. Experience told them that, as they became more exhausted, their resolve to continue would ebb away. On one previous trip to the Arctic, finding it hard to keep up with Fiennes, Stroud had become so desperate to stop that he fantasized about killing his partner. Such was the trust and friendship between them that, after the journey was over, both men could talk freely about it without animosity. They regarded it as a useful insight into the irrational thought processes of exhausted men. Now, their friendship was once again about to be tested to the limit.

Part of the success of their partnership lay in the confidence each man had in the other's strengths and abilities. Fiennes was a skilled navigator, with a wealth of experience and an iron determination. Stroud had an expert knowledge of the human body under stress. Each admired the other's drive and resilience – but, as Fiennes remarked, even 'two saintly monks' would probably fall out in such circumstances.

Early on, they made two decisions that were to cause dreadful hardship later in the journey. In an effort to save weight, when progress was good and the weather mild, they discarded rations and extra layers of warm clothing. But all too soon, pulling heavy weights, trudging through sludgy snow, enduring the fierce rays of the Antarctic sun, and suffering from intense cold and fierce winds all caught up with them.

Their feet were especially affected. Frostbite brought extreme pain. Sores on their heels turned into blisters, and in turn into festering ulcers. Although they carried antibiotics to help treat such problems, these had unfortunate side effects. In the howling gales, they suffered the agony of churning guts for hours, until they could stand it no longer and would have to unbutton their padded overalls, and squat down in the snow. Doing this in the open chilled their bodies to the core and carried a further risk of frostbite.

The thermos flask they used to carry soup in became contaminated, inflicting additional torment on their intestines. Their bodies were unable to digest food properly and they each ended up losing a third of their weight. First, they used up any excess fat, which had acted as insulation against the fierce cold. Then, their muscles began to waste away too. By the time they reached the South Pole, they were burning up 8,000 calories a day, but only eating 5,500.

Most of the journey was made on foot, as it was often too windy, bumpy or dangerous because of crevasses to use the para-sails. Walking drained their waning physical strength, and added greatly to their blisters and ulcers, although it did at least keep them warm. When they could use the sails, it was much quicker and used less of their energy, but they felt colder. The sail harnesses chafed too, injuring their shoulders and backs.

Christmas Day was a low point. As they drank thick, lukewarm soup – fatty to give them extra energy – they both reflected glumly on what their own families would be eating. Fiennes presented Stroud with a huge chocolate bar as a gift. Stroud, touched and surprised by this gesture, wolfed it down, but felt guilty that he'd not thought to bring anything for Fiennes.

It was at this stage, that the two began to realize they'd underestimated how much food they'd need. Their daily rations weren't giving them enough energy for the demands of the trip, and they felt perpetually hungry, ill and depressed.

Stroud began to fantasize about faking serious illness to make Fiennes call the whole thing off. Fiennes was despondent too, but as leader of the expedition, he was liable for the cost of any air rescue. He already had serious money problems at home, so wanting to avoid additional costs gave him extra incentive to complete the expedition.

Fifty four days into the trip, Stroud had another bout of digestive trouble. Too weak to continue, he told Fiennes he needed to rest. He was hurt and surprised when Fiennes became angry with him. The two men put up their tent in strained silence, and Stroud took some medicine and slept for several hours. When he woke, feeling much better, Fiennes told him that he'd decided to continue the journey alone once they'd reached the Pole.

"This is the second time we've had to stop for you," Fiennes said. "If you can't take it, I'm not going to wait."

On day 68, they reached the South Pole. Here, at the Pole itself – marked, in a tongue-in-cheek way, by a large, silver bauble on a striped barber's pole – they met a group of American women who'd walked there. Fiennes and Stroud, happy to meet and talk to other people, set up their tent and offered tea to their new friends. Seeing their filthy, porridge-encrusted cups, the women declined, but they sat together happily, swapping stories.

Fiennes now suggested that Stroud could take a plane out with minimal expense. Stroud was astounded, and very angry. Fiennes apologized, saying he'd been frustrated at being held back by Stroud's stomach problems.

Nowadays, there are research and accommodation buildings close to the Pole, complete with showers, hot food, books and company – all the things Fiennes and Stroud longed for. But the South Pole base has a policy of not supporting independent adventurers. They feel such expeditions are dangerous and should not be encouraged, although they're always prepared to assist and rescue in an emergency. Besides, this was an 'unsupported' attempt, which meant no help in any way from anyone. Stroud, especially, felt quite tearful as they packed up their tent and walked away from this oasis of human habitation.

Soon after their brief stop at the Pole, the two men encountered a strange and unsettling phenomenon. Walking over an area of thin, flat ice, they often plunged six inches down to another layer. Unnervingly, it felt like the start of a fall into a crevasse. Sometimes, triggered by their footsteps, the ice around them would break up and drop down to the layer below. When this happened, it made a colossal noise, like a jet plane approaching.

The second half of the journey was possibly even worse than the first. The Antarctic winter began to take a hold. As colder, stormier weather became more frequent, the chances of a prompt emergency air rescue, should they need it, became less likely. Fiennes had frostbite in his foot, which got worse, but he gritted his teeth and tried to ignore the pain. Stroud lost both his ski sticks, so Fiennes generously gave him one of his.

Then, 81 days into the journey, Stroud fell and fractured his ankle. This led to arguments. Fiennes's frustration was understandable. Frequently having to stop for up to ten minutes to allow Stroud to catch up with him, Fiennes would be almost freezing to death by the time they could begin walking again.

By now, both men were bags of bones. When they rested, sleep was difficult to find. Frostbitten hands and feet, numb during the day, would thaw and ache painfully and insistently. Stroud's hands were so raw, he couldn't bear the thought of taking his gloves on and off. Fiennes's left foot was now so bad that his toes had merged into one grotesque, black, fluid-filled bag, from which oozed a repulsive, stinking liquid. Afterwards he wrote that, when his feet were like that, he would rather have been tortured than have to put on his boots.

Nonetheless, they battled on, but now starvation began to take hold. They both fantasized wildly about food. Each night, they eyed each other warily, to make sure neither got a mouthful more than the other. Even so, they politely took turns to lick the spoon and mug of every last scrap of food.

On day 91, shortly after Fiennes had fallen through a snow-covered crevasse up to his chest, they reached the Ross Ice Shelf. They could now claim to have crossed the Antarctic continent. But the ocean itself, beyond this stretch of sea ice, was still another 580km (360 miles) further north. They pressed on, intending to complete their route to the Scott Base. But then Stroud began to suffer from delirium, the effect of severe hypothermia (loss of body heat), and Fiennes's rotting, frost-bitten feet were causing him constant agony. It was time to call it off. They were 96 days into their trip, and 400km (250 miles) short of their final intended destination.

Fiennes set up their tent and called up a rescue plane on his radio. They were lucky with the weather and were told they'd be picked up within a few hours. Now their supplies no longer needed to last, they ate as if there was no tomorrow: Stroud ate 12 chocolate bars in three hours.

Afterwards, Fiennes reckoned that, had they continued, they would both have died somewhere on the Ross Ice Shelf. In the days that followed, their bodies succumbed to extreme exhaustion. Their limbs swelled up, and they had to be helped on and off planes. When they didn't sleep, they ate.

Both Fiennes and Stroud wrote books about their adventure. Neither made any secret of their animosities and arguments. They'd been immensely courageous in their determination to carry on through extreme suffering. Perhaps it's surprising they didn't quarrel more.

Stroud and Fiennes both finish their accounts of

the trip on a conciliatory note. Stroud writes that some of Fiennes's conduct 'made me spit', but he also said that he would gladly go on another expedition with him. Fiennes might have compared Stroud to 'a crotchety old woman', but he also spoke openly of his admiration for him, and quoted Captain Oates: "When a man is having a hard time, he says hard things about other people which he would regret afterwards."

The two men remain friends.

In 2003, they ran seven marathons in seven days across seven different countries across the world.

GLOSSARY

Antarctica Also known as the Antarctic. Huge frozen
continent at the bottom of the world.

Antarctic circle An imaginary circle around the earth on
a map, at latitude 66° south.

Arctic Huge frozen ocean at the top of the world.

Arctic circle An imaginary circle around the earth on a
map, at latitude 66° north.

blizzard An extreme snowstorm.

crevasse A deep crack or hole in thick ice, especially in
a glacier.

Eskimo An old-fashioned word for the people who live in
the Arctic.

frostbite A medical condition in which parts of the body
become frozen and can be irreparably damaged.

glacier A large river of ice, usually flowing down from
a mountain.

iceberg A large chunk of ice floating in the sea, which has
broken away from a glacier or ice shelf.

ice floe A free-floating block of flat ice in the sea.

ice shelf A layer of thick ice attached to a large bay.

Inuit People who live in the northern polar region, especially of Canada and Greenland. Inuit is used for the plural, and Inuk for the singular.

kayak A small Inuit canoe made from animal bones and skin.

latitude Horizontal lines on a map which divide the world. The North Pole is at latitude 90° north and the South Pole is at latitude 90° south.

longitude Vertical lines on a map which divide the world. All lines of longitude meet up at the North and South Poles.

manhauling Pulling sleds without the aid of animals or windpower.

North Pole The northernmost point on Earth.

Northwest Passage A route from Europe to China and Japan, via the north coast of North America.

pemmican Dried meat or fish mixed with fat, cereals and vegetables to make a nutritious, hard, cake-like bar.

scurvy A deadly disease caused by lack of Vitamin C.

specimen An item collected for medical of scientific study.

South Pole The southernmost point on Earth.

Visit the Usborne Quicklinks website for links to websites where you can step inside Scott's hut in the Antarctic, follow Shackleton's journey and browse photo galleries and online exhibits about other polar expeditions.

Go to **www.usborne.com/quicklinks** and type in the keywords 'Polar Adventures'. Please follow the online safety guidelines at Usborne Quicklinks.